myFocus READER

LEVEL

E

Pearson Education, Inc. 330 Hudson Street, New York, NY 10013

© Pearson Education, Inc. or its affiliates. All Rights Reserved. Printed in the United States of America.

ISBN-13: 978-0-328-99406-9
ISBN-10: 0-328-99406-5

4   19

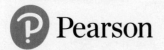

Glenview, Illinois   Boston, Massachusetts
Chandler, Arizona   New York, New York

Contents

Networks

Essential Question

How can a place affect how we live?

PEARSON
realize™
Go ONLINE for all lessons.
myFocus READER

Read and Interact with Text
Develop comprehension and vocabulary. Make connections.

An Amazing Expedition

Weekly Question How can visiting new places expand our understanding of our place in the world?

Comprehension Author's purpose

Academic Vocabulary Synonyms

A Surprise Discovery

Weekly Question In what ways can a place enrich our lives?

Comprehension Questions

Academic Vocabulary Synonyms

A Visit to Space Camp

Weekly Question What can living in outer space teach us about the human body?

Comprehension Text structure

Academic Vocabulary Context clues

A Big Move

Weekly Question What are the advantages of living in different places?

Comprehension Predictions

Academic Vocabulary Synonyms

Solutions in Nature

Weekly Question How can people influence the places where they live?

Comprehension Text structure

Academic Vocabulary Connotation and Denotation

An Amazing Expedition

Explorer Sir Ernest Shackleton would not give up. On December 5, 1914, he and twenty-eight men set out on a ship called *Endurance*. They hoped to reach Antarctica. They wanted to become the first people to cross the land on foot.

They knew there would be a severe winter ahead. Yet they left for Antarctica anyway. Just two days later, the ship ran into pack ice. For the next six weeks, the ship wove through large sections of ice.

On January 18, 1915, the ship was one day from landing. It hit another thick pack ice. By the next morning, ice had trapped the ship on all sides. Shackleton soon realized the ship was stuck. It would stay that way all winter. During this time, Shackleton and his crew were exposed to the harsh weather. Still, they stayed strong.

Nine months later, the crew was still on board. In October 1915, pressure from the ice began to hurt the ship. The ship began to slowly sink. Shackleton and his crew left the ship and made a camp on the ice. On November 21, 1915, *Endurance* sank completely.

The crew camped on the ice for several months. In April 1916, the ice broke in half, causing the crew to flee in lifeboats. Days later, they landed on Elephant Island, about 350 miles from where the *Endurance* sank.

Academic Vocabulary

The word *exposed* means to be put at risk of something. It can also mean "revealed" or "uncovered." Which definition seems to fit best here?

Shackleton knew he had to take a significant step if they were ever to be rescued. Elephant Island was too far away for a rescue attempt. So, a group of six men set off in a lifeboat for South Georgia Island.

The lifeboat landed on the west side of South Georgia Island in May 1916. There were two whaling stations there, but they were on the east side. Shackleton and two others left on foot to travel the twenty-two miles to them.

After thirty hours, the men made it to a whaling station. Finally, on August 30, 1916, the crew was rescued from Elephant Island. After almost two years, the nightmare was over. Not one crew member had died. It was an amazing expedition. It had a happy ending because of one man's determination to bring everyone home safely.

Academic Vocabulary

The root word *signify* means "to be a sign of something." How does that help you understand the word *significant*?

Explain Author's Purpose

Find text evidence on this page to support the idea that Shackleton thought he and his crew members would not survive. What does this tell you about why the author wrote the text?

Unlock the Meaning of the Text

Explain Author's Purpose Reread the text. Think about if the author is writing to inform you about a topic, to tell a story, or to persuade you. Is the text based on a real event?

Academic Vocabulary What does the word *severe* mean in the second paragraph? Try replacing it with a word that means the same thing to help figure out its meaning.

How can visiting new places expand our understanding of our place in the world? Work with a group to discuss how reading about Shackleton's Antarctic expedition helps you understand how new places bring new ideas.

A SURPRISING DISCOVERY

Academic Vocabulary

Look for the root word *sign* in *significant* to help you figure out its meaning. *Sign* has many meanings; here it means to show something.

Academic Vocabulary

The affix *con-* in the word *contribute* means "together." How does knowing the affix help you understand the word's meaning?

"Marcus, get your mother!" Aldo yelled. "I have something to show her!" It was a really hot day. Aldo had risen early. He and his son wanted to work in the coolness of the morning. They raised olives and grapes on a small farm in Italy in the early 1700s. These crops grew well in the fertile soil, because of the volcanic ash.

That morning Aldo was digging a new well. As he was digging, his shovel hit something hard. He put the shovel down. Then he started scraping at the dirt with his hands. When Marcus returned with his mother, they found Aldo looking into the eyes of a face. They helped him dig down deep. Finally, the rest of the object was fully exposed. They had uncovered an entire statue carved from marble. It was a significant find.

"Aldo, my sister told me about a neighbor who found something like this when he dug his well," Mother said. "Do you think this goes together with it?"

The family met with their neighbors. Soon everyone was comparing items they had found in their fields. People had dug up coins, jewelry, bowls, and bricks. Some had even found bones.

"These artifacts will contribute to our knowledge of the past," said Aldo.

Aldo and his neighbors worked their lands. They uncovered many other great artifacts buried in the soil. Soon, however, they were told to stop. They found out their farms were located on a special site. It was near where the ancient city of Herculaneum had once been. To continue digging might hurt the ruins.

Many centuries earlier, Herculaneum and Pompeii had been great cities. Yet one terrible day in A.D. 79, a volcanic eruption took place. The nearby volcano known as Mount Vesuvius (ve SUE vee es) erupted. It buried these two cities under rock and ash. Thousands of people died. Everything in the cities was burned or buried.

Historians and archaeologists from all over the world have come to the area. They wanted to dig to see what they could find. Tourists come to these cities each year to see the ruins.

Generate Questions

What questions do you have about why Aldo was told to stop digging? Write down your questions and see if you can find answers in the text.

Unlock the Meaning of the Text

Generate Questions Go back to the text. Reread each paragraph and then write a question about what you read. Find a partner and ask each other the questions you wrote to make sure you understood the story.

Academic Vocabulary Go back to reread the second paragraph. Find the word *exposed*. How do the words *fully* and *uncovered* help you to figure out its meaning?

In what ways can a place enrich our lives? With a small group, talk about how the text helps you understand how new places can help us see the world differently. Discuss a place that made your life richer after reading about it or visiting it.

A Visit to Space Camp

Analyze Text Structure

The first paragraph states the main idea. What is the main idea of the passage?

Have you ever looked up at the sky and thought about what space is like? Imagine putting on a spacesuit and blasting off into space. This may seem like a dream. Yet the National Aeronautics and Space Administration (NASA) gives kids a significant chance to see what it is like in space.

Camp Kennedy Space Center is a summer camp that lasts one week. It is held at the Kennedy Space Center in Florida. Campers from grades two to eleven can go. They enjoy space fun and adventure.

Academic Vocabulary

The word *severe* has multiple meanings. What meaning makes the most sense in this sentence?

Campers see and feel what it is like to be an astronaut. They see what it is like to explore in space, too. They learn how human bodies are protected from the severe coldness of space. Students work in teams to study the future of space travel. They also design space vehicles. They even meet real astronauts! Campers can ask them questions about their work and habits in space.

Academic Vocabulary

The Latin root of *habit* is *habitus*, which means "style or practice." How does the meaning of the root help you understand the meaning of *habit*?

Campers feel what it's like to be on space vehicles. They also get to see what it is like to be weightless. After all, there is no gravity in space. Astronauts can't stay on the ground in space! Campers even find out how different it can be to eat in space. Our bodies are not made for eating without gravity.

Perhaps the best part of space camp is stepping into the Shuttle Launch Experience®. Inside, a former space shuttle commander briefs visitors about the steps of a space shuttle launch. They go right up to the final countdown. Three, two, one, blast off! Campers get the sound and lighting effects that are like those on a real space shuttle launch.

Campers at Camp Kennedy Space Center have a lot of fun. They learn a lot, too. Each year, NASA hopes the camp will encourage kids to want to become astronauts.

Unlock the Meaning of the Text

Analyze Text Structure The author structures the text as main idea and detail. Find two details that support the main idea. Explain how they support the main idea.

Academic Vocabulary Find the word *significant* in the first paragraph. Use the context to help you determine its meaning.

What can living in outer space teach us about the human body? With a partner, discuss how reading this helps you understand what space can teach us. What other things can living in space teach us?

A Big Move

Make and Confirm Predictions

How does the title help you to predict what you will be reading about? Continue reading and confirm or change your prediction.

Academic Vocabulary

In this sentence, what words help you to understand what *habit* means?

Academic Vocabulary

In this sentence, the word *significant* means "very important." What synonyms could you use for *significant* in this sentence?

Shelly's mom came into the living room and quietly turned off the TV. She motioned for Shelly to follow her into the kitchen. "We have some significant things to talk about," Mom said. Shelly dreaded the sound of this because "significant things" usually meant bad news.

Nervously, she followed her mother to the kitchen where her father was already seated at the table. It was his habit to sit and read the newspaper there every night after dinner.

Dad broke the silence. "We have some exciting news. I've accepted a new job, so we'll be moving. The job is in Israel."

It was a severe blow to Shelly. Her stomach sank and her mouth dropped open. "I don't want to move!" she cried.

"I know, Shelly, but this is a significant opportunity for your dad. It's also a great chance for our family to learn the customs of another country," continued Mom. "It will be a huge change for all of us. Some of our habits will change."

"When are we moving?" Shelly asked between sobs.

"We won't move until the end of the school year. You can finish fourth grade and start your next school year in Israel."

Shelly had heard enough. She ran to her bedroom, flung herself on the bed, and cried into her pillow.

To get ready, Shelly's parents told her what life would be like in her new home. They found a place to live and a school for Shelly. They even got the name of a girl, Hadara, who would be in Shelly's class.

Shelly sent an email to Hadara, asking her a lot of questions about what her life would be like in Israel. Hadara promised to help Shelly learn the Hebrew language and show her how much fun she would have in her new country.

Finally, it was the end of the school year. The week before she left, Shelly's friends threw her a surprise going-away party. They told her how much they would miss her, and they gave her a teddy bear to hug if she felt homesick.

As she sat with her parents on the airplane, Shelly had mixed feelings. She hugged her teddy bear and thought of her friends waiting for her first email from Israel. Then Shelly remembered Hadara and smiled. She already had one new friend waiting for her.

Unlock the Meaning of the Text

Make and Confirm Predictions Based on the end of the story, how do you predict Shelly will feel about living in a new country?

Academic Vocabulary Find the word *severe* in the fourth paragraph. What is a synonym of *severe* that you could use in this sentence?

What are the advantages of living in different places? With a partner, discuss a time when you or someone you know moved. What were some advantages of the move? Share how reading this story helped you connect to that memory.

Solutions in Nature

Analyze Text Structure

Authors often use main idea and details as a text structure. How do you know this text follows that structure?

An invention is a way to solve a problem. Being able to solve problems can be the difference between life and death for living things. Animals, plants, and microbes have found many ways to adapt on Earth.

Today, scientists in the field of biomimicry look to the natural world to solve problems. The word comes from *bio-*, meaning "life." *Mimic* means "to imitate." Look at the Wright brothers. They watched birds fly, which gave them significant ideas about how to make airplanes.

Some bacteria live only in oil pipelines. Bacteria get energy and food by breaking down oil. Engineers now use these bacteria to clean pipelines and the tanks where oil is stored. They also use bacteria to clean up oil spills.

The way that butterfly wings are made can push dirt away and cause water to roll off. Engineers copy that structure when they make paints and cloths that resist dirt.

Many kinds of insects have wings shaped like panels to take in energy from the sun. The wings move air in ways that help the insect to fly better. A sailboat copies this design to use wind and sun energy. These two kinds of energy are abundant, and using them is good for Earth.

Butterfly wings provide a model for dirt-resistant paints and textiles.

Tree trunks have fibers that are exposed to the flow of forces acting on them. Because of this, tree trunks do not break easily. So, engineers have tried to copy this structure. They have used it to build cars that are light but tough. Cars using this design are as safe as other cars. Yet, they are much lighter.

Biomimicry has led to many inventions that make clean energy. One example is bioWAVE-units. They are placed on the ocean floor and change wave motion into electricity. These units copy the way seaweed looks and moves.

Plants and animals have helped people in so many ways. So, the next time you need to solve a problem, look outside!

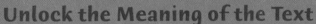

Seaweed motion contributes to the development of sustainable energies.

A sailboat design mimics the wings of insects.

Academic Vocabulary

How would adding a different affix, such as *im-*, change the meaning of the word *exposed*?

Academic Vocabulary

In the caption above, the word *contributes* could be replaced with what related word?

Unlock the Meaning of the Text

Analyze Text Structure Choose two paragraphs and write the main idea and the details that support each idea. How does this help you see the main-ideas-and-details text structure more clearly?

Academic Vocabulary Find the word *significant* in the second paragraph. The connotation of *significant* is "having value or importance." Look up the denotation of the word in the dictionary and compare the two meanings.

How can people influence the places where they live? With a partner, discuss how reading the text helped you learn about people influencing the places where they live by what they do.

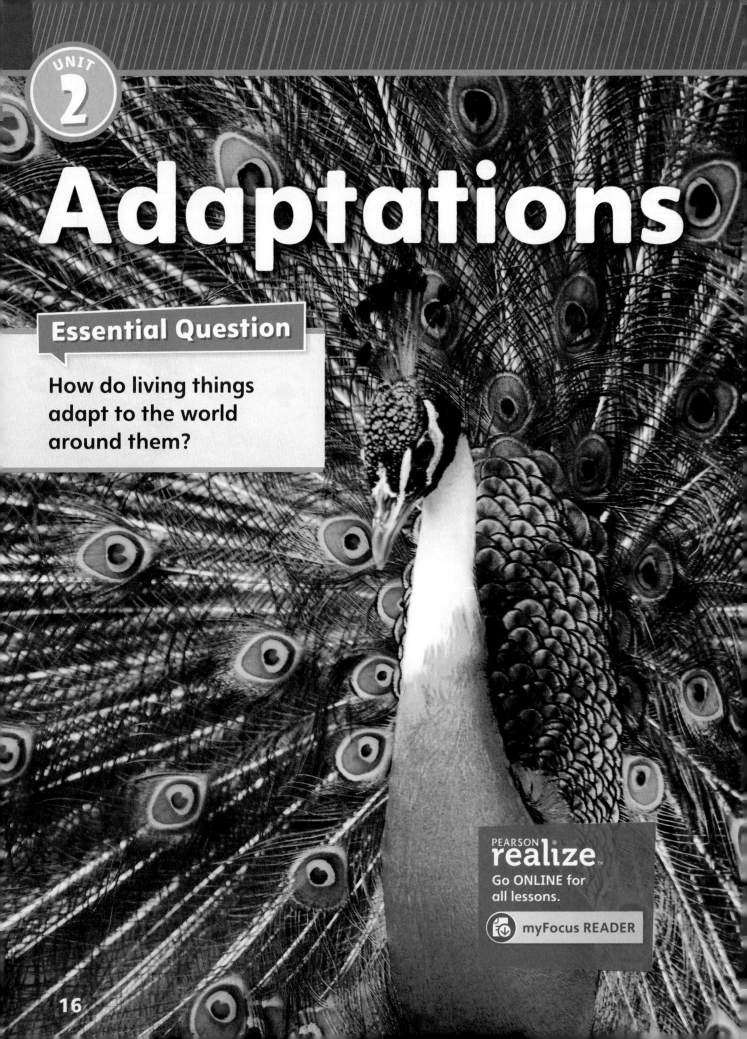

Adaptations

Essential Question

How do living things adapt to the world around them?

PEARSON
realize
Go ONLINE for all lessons.

myFocus READER

Read and Interact with Text
Develop comprehension and vocabulary. Make connections.

A Special Breed of Dog

Weekly Question What different purposes do animal adaptations serve?
Comprehension Text structure
Academic Vocabulary Context clues

The Artic Tern's Amazing Journey

Weekly Question How do adaptations help animals survive?
Comprehension Text feature
Academic Vocabulary Context clues

Desert Creatures

Weekly Question What challenges do animals face in their environments?
Comprehension Setting and plot
Academic Vocabulary Synonyms

How to Raise Puppies

Weekly Question In what ways do living things depend on each other?
Comprehension Visualization
Academic Vocabulary Context clues

Animals in Disguise

Weekly Question How do adaptations make animals unique?
Comprehension Information
Academic Vocabulary Shades of meaning

A Special Breed of Dog

Alano Español

More than 1,600 years ago, a group of people called the Alans moved to the country we now call Spain. The Alans came from very far away, near what is now the country of Iran. People from other lands made them leave that area. The Alans moved across Europe and they brought their dogs with them. The people of Spain liked these dogs. When the Spanish people went to new lands, they also took these dogs with them.

This breed, or type, of dog is called Alano Español, which means "Spanish bulldog." These dogs are very large. They have big, square heads, just like bulldogs. Their front legs are very strong, and they have large paws. Their fur is short and thick, which helps them survive in any kind of weather.

These dogs do not bark very much. But they do listen to their owners and follow what they are told to do. The dogs are not friendly to strangers, but they love the people who own them. This makes them very good guard dogs. Their owners count on the dogs for defense. They protect their owners and keep their homes and lands safe.

Academic Vocabulary

The word *survive* means "to live through something." What is a synonym that you could use to replace the word *survive*?

Academic Vocabulary

A word's connotation is the feelings associated with it. What is the connotation of *defense*?

These big, strong dogs can run for a long time without getting tired. This helps them work with cattle, to move them from place to place. Spanish bulldogs also help their owners hunt. Spanish bulldogs have strong jaws. They can hold on to wild animals. Some Spanish bulldogs have even helped their owners to fight in wars.

Long ago, the Spanish bulldog could be found in many parts of Europe. But then this breed seemed to die out and was found only in Spain. Now these bulldogs have come to North America. Dog breeders have brought them over from Spain for people who are looking to acquire a special breed.

Spanish bulldogs still work hard to protect their owners. They continue to work with cattle and hunt with their owners. The Alano Español is a very special breed of dog!

Analyze Main Idea and Detail

The author says that Spanish bulldogs are a special breed. What details support this idea?

Unlock the Meaning of the Text

Analyze Main Idea and Details When you analyze the main idea and details, you go back to reread the text closely to determine how the details support the main idea. List three details that support the main idea of the passage.

Academic Vocabulary Reread paragraph five. What does the word *acquire* mean? What clues helped you figure out the meaning?

What different purposes do animal adaptations serve? With a partner, discuss what unique features and skills the Alano Español breed has that make them useful dogs to their owners.

The Alano Español is not the only type of dog that is good for herding. Other breeds, such as the border collie, are fantastic herders.

The Arctic Tern's Amazing Journey

Analyze Text Structure

One type of text structure is main idea and detail. What is the main idea of this passage? What details in the first three paragraphs support this main idea?

Academic Vocabulary

In this sentence, *classified* means "sorted by class or by type." Can you think of another meaning for *classified*?

Academic Vocabulary

How are the words *survivor* and *survival* related to *survive*? How do the suffixes *-or* and *-al* change the meaning of the base word *survive*?

Each year, Arctic terns make a very long trip. These birds fly to the North Pole every spring. They spend the summer there to lay eggs and raise their young. They fly to the South Pole every fall, where they spend the winter. That's a trip of more than 21,000 miles each year!

Arctic terns are classified as members of the gull family. They are medium-sized birds with white feathers on their heads and long tails. They also have webbed feet. This helps them dive into the water to catch the small fish they eat.

No other bird flies as far as the Arctic tern does each year. Many other birds migrate, which means to move from one place to another at different seasons. They fly from a place with cold winter weather to a place with warm winter weather. This helps them survive the winter. In warm weather, birds can find food that can be hard to find in cold weather.

Some birds migrate even if it is warm all year. Sometimes there is not enough water in the dry season in Africa. Then birds will fly to other places that have more rain.

Birds use natural landmarks like bodies of water to help them find their way. Arctic terns leave their nests in the north and fly south along the coast toward Antarctica. Scientists believe birds have an acquired sense of when it's time to migrate and where they need to go.

Arctic terns have two summers each year. They spend long summer days near the North Pole. Then they fly south for the long summer days near the South Pole. Arctic terns see more daylight hours than any other animal on Earth.

In June, July, and August, Arctic terns live in the Arctic. Then they spend three months flying south. In December, January, and February, they live in the Antarctic. After that, they spend three months flying north. They do this over and over again, for years and years!

Unlock the Meaning of the Text

Analyze Text Structure Find places where the author uses description, compare-and-contrast, and sequence text structures. How do these text structures help you understand the main idea of the passage?

Academic Vocabulary Find the word *acquired* in the first paragraph on this page. Use the context to help you state the meaning of *acquired*.

How do adaptations help animals survive? With a partner, discuss how this text helps you understand why animals adapt and how adaptation helps them survive in a harsh environment.

Desert Creatures

Analyze Setting and Plot

A story's setting is where and when it takes place. What is the setting of this story? How do you think it will affect the plot?

Academic Vocabulary

The Latin root word *viv* means "live" or "life." How does it help you understand the meaning of the word *survive*?

It was like any other regular night in New Mexico. The air was cool and dry, and the stars were shining bright in the sky. Only one thing made this night different from the others. A meeting was being held, and all the desert creatures were there. Each one took a turn to speak.

Black Widow Spider was the first to speak up. "The desert can be a scary, dangerous place, so we must be able to defend ourselves," the spider said. "I can spin a sticky web. If something attacks me, I can rush forward and inject poison into it. I can even suck out the liquid from inside of my victim's body. What can the rest of you do to survive?"

The rest of the desert creatures thought about what they could do to defend themselves if attacked.

"Everyone's afraid of monsters!" said Gila Monster proudly. "Instead of basking in the sun, I'll sneak up on intruders. Then, with one big bite, they'll be stopped."

Fire Ant spoke up next, saying, "When something attacks me, I call upon my army of ants. We are always ready to fight.

We can swarm on our enemies and then bite and sting them! We might be little, but we have sufficient skills!"

Then Rattlesnake spoke up. "I usually like to keep to myself," said the snake. "But to survive, I quickly slither back and forth. Then I sink my sharp teeth into anything that comes too close."

Then Tarantula spoke up, saying, "Unlike other spiders, I don't trap my prey in a sticky web. Instead, I use my large legs to grab them and then attack them with my sharp fangs. Then I inject poison inside of them. It's my best defense!"

African Honeybee buzzed into the meeting. The bee was just returning from an African safari. The small bee spoke up. "My colony knows how to keep me safe. We have poisoned more enemies than all of you combined. We will gladly remove any threat," buzzed African Honeybee.

The meeting ended with everyone knowing they could defend themselves. Then they all had a restful and safe night's sleep.

Academic Vocabulary

What topic are the creatures speaking about? How does this context help you understand the word *defense*?

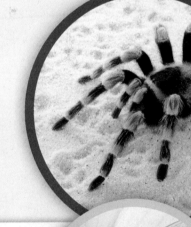

Unlock the Meaning of the Text

Analyze Plot and Setting Analyze the plot and setting and determine how they work together. How would the story change if the setting changed?

Academic Vocabulary Look at the word *sufficient* in the first paragraph on this page. What do you think it means to have *sufficient* skills? What synonym can you use to replace the word *sufficient*?

What challenges do animals face in their environments? With a partner, discuss how this story helps you understand the challenges animals face in the desert.

How to Raise PUPPIES

24

Academic Vocabulary

Synonyms for the word *acquire* include *develop*, *gain*, and *learn*. In this sentence, what does *acquire* mean?

Visualize

How do the details in this paragraph help you to visualize what the puppies learn in obedience class?

Do you love puppies? Have you ever thought of raising them? Puppy Raisers help puppies to be Seeing Eye dogs.

A Seeing Eye dog is a dog that helps people who cannot see. These dogs also help people with other visual challenges. Seeing Eye dogs are also called guide dogs. After they acquire the right training, these dogs can guide their masters anywhere. The dogs take them around busy sidewalks and streets. They can lead their owners through crowded malls and airports.

As a Puppy Raiser, your family gets a puppy when it's about eight weeks old. Your job is to foster the puppy. You give it a good home until it's about eighteen months old. During that time, you must spend a lot of time with the puppy. Take the puppy almost everywhere you go! The puppy needs to get used to being around people in many different places, even loud and busy ones!

You must take the puppy to obedience classes. At the classes, the puppy learns how to follow commands like *sit*, *stay*, and *come*. Puppies learn special skills too.

Some of these skills are learning to lie down on command and walk on a leash. Your job is to practice with the puppy until it is an expert in all of these skills.

After about a year and a half, the puppy heads off to more training. This is where it learns to be a Seeing Eye dog. This training will get the dog ready for a new owner. The owner will be a visually challenged person who will rely on the dog to help make life easier.

So do you want to be a Puppy Raiser? First, your parents must fill out an application and answer questions. If your family passes, you will receive a puppy. You will also get all the things your puppy needs, including a sufficient supply of food, a dish, a leash, and toys. Then you can enjoy training the new puppy. When the puppy moves on to do its job, you can always foster another puppy!

Academic Vocabulary

What affix could you add to *sufficient* to make it an antonym of *sufficient*?

Unlock the Meaning of the Text

Visualize When you visualize the details in a text, you use the author's descriptions to see pictures in your mind. What details does the author use to help you visualize what it's like to be a Puppy Raiser?

Academic Vocabulary Read the sentence in the second paragraph in which the word *acquire* appears. With a partner, discuss other things that you or other living things can acquire.

In what ways do living things depend on each other? With a partner, discuss how owners depend on Seeing Eye dogs. How do the dogs depend on Puppy Raisers?

Animals in Disguise

Life can be difficult for some animals. Imagine spending most of your life either looking for food or trying to not to become food yourself! For most animals, both of these tasks are necessary.

Academic Vocabulary

Some words have similar meanings. How does the meaning of the word *defense* relate to the word *protection*?

But what can animals do? How does a lion sneak up on its prey without being seen? What defense can insects use to not become a snack for birds? How do little fish protect themselves when bigger fish try to eat them? It doesn't matter if an animal is classified as a predator or as prey. Being able to "disappear" into their surroundings can help animals stay alive.

An animal can take on the look of its environment. For example, lions seem to fade into the tall grass of the savanna. That way, they can sneak up on their prey without being spotted. Squirrel fur is rough, uneven, and a gray-brown color. A squirrel looks like tree bark to a hawk or an eagle searching for food. Some insects have a hard shell that looks like dead leaves or branches.

Some animals can camouflage themselves. This means they can change color to match the background as they move from place to place. This makes them almost invisible to their predators.

Some sea creatures change color when they eat. Think about being the color of the food you ate for lunch! Imagine what it would be like to be able to do that!

Birds can't change color quickly. But many do change color with the seasons. Different temperatures cause these birds to grow a new set of feathers. The hours of daylight also affect feather color. A bird may be mostly brown in summer. But it may have feathers that are white as snow in winter!

Developing camouflage comes from the process called natural selection. If an animal's coloring closely matches its surroundings, then predators are less likely to catch it. With this adaptation, an animal can survive to produce offspring. Then the offspring are born with the same adaptation. That means they also can live long enough to pass it on.

The next time you're outside, look around very closely. You never know what might be looking back at you!

Synthesize Information

How is the way sea creatures change color different from the way some birds change color?

Academic Vocabulary

A form of the word *survive* appears earlier in the text. In which paragraph does it appear and what form of *survive* is used?

Unlock the Meaning of the Text

Synthesize Information When you synthesize, you need to look closely at two or more things and combine them to create something new. What information can you synthesize about how predators use camouflage and how it is used by prey?

Academic Vocabulary The word *classified* is the past tense of the word *classify*. How does knowing this form of the word help you understand its meaning?

How do adaptations make animals unique? With a partner, discuss how the text helps you see that adaptations such as camouflage make animals special. Then discuss special abilities or skills that make you unique.

Diversity

Essential Question

How can we reach new understandings through exploring diversity?

PEARSON
realize™
Go ONLINE for
all lessons.

 myFocus READER

Read and Interact with Text
Develop comprehension and vocabulary. Make connections.

Native American Heroes
Weekly Question Why do people communicate in diverse ways?
Comprehension Inferences
Academic Vocabulary Root words and affixes

A Circus for All
Weekly Question How do our experiences help us see the world differently?
Comprehension Predictions
Academic Vocabulary Context clues

Making Music Together
Weekly Question How does music bring people together?
Comprehension Author's purpose
Academic Vocabulary Multiple-meaning words

A Visit to a New Place
Weekly Question How do new places influence us?
Comprehension Point of view
Academic Vocabulary Root words and affixes

A New Classmate
Weekly Question How do people with interests different from ours help us grow?
Comprehension Visualization
Academic Vocabulary Context clues

Native American Heroes

Make Inferences

Why do you think it was important for to give the Navajo Code Talkers recognition and awards for their service during World War II?

Synonyms

Words like *clash*, *dispute*, *fight*, and *struggle* can all be synonyms for *conflict*. How do these synonyms help you understand the meaning of the word?

On July 26, 2001, four Native Americans received the Congressional Gold Medal in Washington, D.C. This medal is the highest award for an American. President George W. Bush gave the medals to the men. He said, "Today, America honors twenty-one Native Americans who, in a desperate hour, gave their country a service only they could give. In war, using their native language, they relayed secret messages that turned the course of battle."

The men were John Brown, Chester Nez, Lloyd Oliver, and Allen Dale June. Another man, Joe Palmer, was also given a medal. But he was too sick to travel. These five men were Marines in World War II. They were also the first Navajo Code Talkers. World War II was one of the biggest conflicts in history. The Code Talkers helped the United States by sending secret messages. They kept the information in the messages safe by speaking in code. The code was based on the Navajo language, Diné.

It took 60 years for the Code Talkers to get their awards. Later that year the U.S. government gave Congressional Silver Medals to more than two hundred Code Talkers. These men had been trained by the first Code Talkers. Later a movie was made about them called *Windtalkers*.

Bill Toledo was one Code Talker who received a silver medal. He joined the Marines after high school. He was a Code Talker from 1942 to 1945. Toledo faced many challenges in the war. He was almost hit by bullets, but he moved quickly and escaped. Then someone thought he was a Japanese soldier. He was taken prisoner at gunpoint. Later he was given a bodyguard so that would not happen again.

Toledo says it's important to tell his story to young people. He wants them to understand that freedom comes at a cost. He wants them to know how Code Talkers served their country when it was in need.

Multiple Meaning

Words *Challenge* can be both a noun and a verb. It can mean "a test of a person's abilities." It can also mean "a dare or a demand for proof." How is the word used in this text?

Unlock the Meaning of the Text

Make Inferences Think about the challenges that the Navajo Code Talkers faced. What do you think their biggest challenges were during the war? Use details from the text and what you already know.

Academic Vocabulary The word *challenge* comes from the Latin *calumnia*, which means "accusation" or "to blame for something." When could a challenge be an accusation? Work with a partner to brainstorm ideas.

Why do people communicate in diverse ways? Talk with a partner about details from the text that show new ways to communicate. Then brainstorm all of the ways you communicate with people.

A CIRCUS FOR ALL

Academic Vocabulary

The word *accomplish* comes from the Latin root *complere*, which means to *complete*. What do you think *accomplish* means in this sentence?

Make and Confirm Predictions

How do you think the circus staff will help new students feel less nervous about the class? What details in the text helped confirm your prediction?

Come one! Come all! The circus is in town!

In Saint Louis, Missouri, a circus is in town every day. It's called Circus Harmony, and it's a fun program for kids of all ages. You don't have to have special skills to join. But you do need to know about teamwork.

Since 2001, Circus Harmony has been teaching children all kinds of circus tricks. Some kids enroll in tumbling classes. Others might learn to ride a unicycle. But along the way, kids accomplish much more. They don't just learn to juggle or build human pyramids. They learn how to connect to each other as they work together, no matter who they are.

One of the main goals of Circus Harmony is very simple. They want kids to learn that people are more alike than they are different. Imagine you are part of a group that will build a human pyramid. It's the first day of class. You look around, feeling nervous. Everyone else looks so calm! You wonder how you're going to fit in. But the staff at Circus Harmony already knows how you're feeling. They also know that everyone else is feeling like you do!

So they begin with some easy warm-ups. They don't want to throw too many challenges at you too soon. They teach you ways to talk to the other students and ways to help them. Pretty soon you're working together to make a pyramid that seems sky-high!

Or suppose you sign up for a trapeze class. There you are in a safety harness. A classmate is close behind you on the platform. He or she holds you tight, waiting for your signal to let go. A month ago you didn't even know this person! Thanks to Circus Harmony, you have learned to trust your classmate.

Circus Harmony performs in front of hundreds of people every year. Some of the students have gone on to participate in popular shows like Cirque du Soleil. Clap your hands for these talented and hard-working people!

Academic Vocabulary

The word *participate* means "to take part in." But there are other ways to say that, such as *join*, *share*, and *cooperate*. How do these synonyms help you understand what it means to *participate* in something?

Unlock the Meaning of the Text

Make and Confirm Predictions
Choose a circus act or skill that you would like to try. In what ways could the teachers at Circus Harmony help you become good at your skill? Share three predictions with a partner.

Academic Vocabulary
A *challenge* can be a test of what a person is able to do. Would you rather have a challenge or take a test? Write down reasons for your answer.

How do our experiences help us see the world differently?
Discuss with a partner how kids might see the world after a class at Circus Harmony. Make a list of details that support your ideas.

Making Music Together

Academic Vocabulary

What suffix could you add to *expand* to make a different form of the word? How does adding a suffix change the meaning of the word?

Academic Vocabulary

What synonym could you use in place of *participate* in this sentence that would not change its meaning?

Explain Author's Purpose

Why do you think the author wrote this text? Think about the details the author gives, including facts about life before the Civil War.

Do you want to go to summer camp but don't want to play sports or explore nature? Would you like to expand what you know about music instead?

Then check out Blues Camp in Chicago! Blues Camp is for young musicians who want to learn about and perform blues music. You must try out to be accepted. But young people from all over the world come to participate in Blues Camp. It opens their minds and ears to a different kind of music. Today, radio stations play mostly hip-hop, rap, country, or rock music. Blues music is very different. Campers say they like hearing the more unfamiliar sounds of the blues.

You don't need to be an expert on the blues on your first day at camp. Guest speakers tell students about some of the most famous blues singers of all time. These singers include Bessie Smith, Muddy Waters, B.B. King, and Etta James. Campers listen to and talk about their songs.

Campers also learn about different blues instruments. These include guitars, drums, horns, harmonicas, pianos, and keyboards.

Some kids are surprised to find out how important the blues are in the history of American music. Campers learn how the blues began in the South before the Civil War conflict. African American enslaved people sang while they worked in the fields. The songs were first known as "field hollers." This was because they called out and responded as they worked. The songs told about being poor, working hard, and having little hope. After the Civil War, many African Americans moved north to cities like Chicago. They shared their music there.

Campers often say they can't wait to share what they have accomplished with family and friends. But campers say the best part of the camp is performing. They present their music at concerts. Campers also get together to play just for fun. What could be better for someone who loves music than a week at Blues Camp?

Unlock the Meaning of the Text

Explain Author's Purpose Look for details that support the author's purpose for writing this text. Is the author's purpose to inform, to explain, or to persuade?

Academic Vocabulary The word *conflict* means "a disagreement between people or groups." A conflict can also be a military battle or fight between two sides. Which definition is used in this text?

How does music bring people together? With a partner, discuss how the text explains how the blues brought African Americans together in the past and how it brings young people together at Blues Camp today.

A Visit to a New Place

Academic Vocabulary

In the third paragraph, *challenge* is a noun meaning "something that is hard to do." Think of experiences that were a *challenge* for you.

Academic Vocabulary

The word *expand* means "to grow bigger." Look at another use of the word on the next page. How are the meanings different?

Leon and Marc were going to Cuba with their dad. "Do you think Cuba will be anything like New York City?" Leon asked his brother.

"I guess we'll find out," Marc replied.

The flight to Havana lasted several hours. Getting through customs seemed to take even longer. Then they had to find a taxi to take them to their Grandmother's apartment. So far, the boys thought the trip was quite a challenge.

The boys stared out the taxi windows. They thought the plants and streets looked strange. Dad tried to cheer them up. "Hey guys, I know this place is quite different from what you're used to. But people are slowly fixing it up. Besides, it's always good to expand your experiences, right?" But all the boys could see were old buildings that needed new paint.

Grandmother's bright yellow building had a bakery shop on the first floor and apartments above it. Grandmother hugged everyone tightly and led them upstairs. "We'll rest tonight," she said. "But tomorrow I'll show you my beautiful city."

The next morning, Grandmother's friend Mel picked them up in his taxi. Mel drove the family down narrow streets in the oldest parts of town. He pointed out huge museums, busy markets, and stone churches. He also told stories about Cuba's history. The boys were interested to learn about the Spanish fort built in the 1500s.

36

Mel dropped the family off at the Fountain of Lions. There, the boys played and danced with other children to the beat of bongo drums. Then Grandmother led them through a maze of open markets and tiny shops. She stopped at a small restaurant where spicy smells filled the air. "Soon you'll be expanding your stomachs as well as your experiences," she joked.

"How do you know about this place?" Marc asked, biting into a tamale.

Grandmother smiled. "I lived here all my life. Would you like to hear some stories about what life was like when I was a young girl?" she asked. The boys nodded, and Grandmother recounted her childhood memories of growing up in Havana.

When it was time to go back to New York, Leon and Marc were sad to leave. Every day with Grandmother had been an adventure. They enjoyed visiting Cuba and learning about its history. But most of all, they had made new memories. Now they couldn't wait to visit Grandmother again!

Point of View

Your point of view is the way you look at or think about something. How does the boys' point of view about Havana change?

Unlock the Meaning of the Text

Point of View Reread what Dad tells the boys in the fourth paragraph. How is his point of view different from Leon and Marc's point of view? How does Dad's point of view influence Leon and Marc?

Academic Vocabulary Find the second use of the word *expand* in the story. What suffix has been added to the word? How does it change the meaning?

How do new places influence us? With a small group, discuss how the text helps you understand how visiting new places can affect us. Then take turns telling about a new place you have visited.

A New Classmate

Visualize

Having a picture in your mind can help you understand a text. How does this classroom look? How is it the same as your classroom?

Everyone in the classroom was talking. Their teacher just told them that a student from Mexico would soon be joining their class. They were excited about the news!

Mrs. Taylor asked everyone to quiet down. "I know you're excited about our new student," she said, "but I have some other good news too."

"The principal and I decided that it would be helpful for us to learn some Spanish so that we can talk more easily with Alma. She can learn English while we learn Spanish," Mrs. Taylor explained.

"I know some Spanish already," said Kelly. "My grandparents speak Spanish."

"Great!" Mrs. Taylor responded. "You can help us learn Spanish, too. We have a Spanish teacher coming today. He's going to teach us some Spanish language basics. Then you'll feel more confident talking with Alma when she comes."

Just then a man walked in and introduced himself. "Hello! I'm Mr. Garza. I know that learning a new language is a challenge, but I have some tips for you. Before you know it, you and Alma will be having a conversation.

"First, you'll want to spend as much time as you can listening to the language. I'm going to leave some Spanish language podcasts for you. That way you can listen and practice saying the words with the speaker.

"Second, it's important to dive right in and participate. I'll be here only twice a week because I have a conflict in my schedule. It's up to you to practice what you are learning and talk to each other!

"The third tip is the most important. Don't worry about making mistakes. You're all in this together! Don't be afraid to ask me or Alma how to say something. The more you participate, the faster you'll learn."

Then Mr. Garza taught the class a few Spanish words and phrases. After he left, some students practiced saying them aloud in small groups. Other students listened to the podcasts that he left for them. They were excited to learn as much as they could because Alma was coming soon!

Academic Vocabulary

A *challenge* is something that is hard to do. What are some synonyms for the word *challenge*?

Academic Vocabulary

The word *participate* means "to take part in." What are two ways the students can participate in learning Spanish?

Unlock the Meaning of the Text

Visualize Describe to a partner how you see the students in Mrs. Taylor's classroom working together to learn Spanish. How does your "mind picture" help you understand the story?

Academic Vocabulary Find the word *conflict* in the text. A conflict can be something that gets in the way. What is another word for *conflict*?

How do people with interests different from ours help us grow? How will Alma's arrival change the students in this classroom? With a partner, talk about a time when a new student or teacher helped your school change or grow.

Impacts

Essential Question

How do our stories shape our world?

Read and Interact with Text
Develop comprehension and vocabulary. Make connections.

Keeping a Secret

Weekly Question How can revealing a secret make it lose its power?

Comprehension Characters

Academic Vocabulary Root words and affixes

The Benefits of Being Different

Weekly Question How can being different be an advantage?

Comprehension Theme

Academic Vocabulary Synonyms

Rewards of a Good Deed

Weekly Question Why should we do good deeds without expecting anything in return?

Comprehension Text Summary

Academic Vocabulary Root words and affixes

A New Twist to an Old Tale

Weekly Question How can what we learn from stories guide our actions?

Comprehension Theme

Academic Vocabulary Synonyms

A Lesson Learned

Weekly Question How can being disobedient cause problems?

Comprehension Details

Academic Vocabulary Root words and affixes

KEEPING A SECRET

Jenna huddled in the backyard, unsuccessfully fighting back the tears running down her face. She had promised her older brother, Adam, that she wouldn't inform anyone about him not going to class. However, Jenna was concerned, Adam's new friends were taking him in a dangerous direction.

Jenna's dad strolled over and asked, "May I join you?" Jenna nodded, and he perched on the bench beside her.

"Everyone knows you're great at keeping secrets, and I admire that," Dad observed. "However, I think keeping things in is hurting you." Jenna just stared at her feet. Dad continued, "It's not difficult to guess you're protecting Adam."

"How could you know?" Jenna blurted out.

"You two have always been close, and you haven't spoken to him for weeks. It's not hard to interpret that behavior," Dad responded.

"I swore I wouldn't say anything," Jenna cried.

"I'm guessing the secret involves his behavior at school," Dad continued.

Jenna was panicked, but she also felt a sense of relief. "I'm glad you know."

"What are your thoughts about Adam's new friends?" Dad asked.

"They are definitely not a good influence on him," Jenna replied.

Dad gave Jenna a big hug. "Tonight, I predict it's going to end."

Academic Vocabulary

Synonyms for the word *interpret* include *understand*, *translate*, and *explain*. How do these synonyms help you understand how the word *interpret* is used in this story?

Analyze Characters

One way authors help readers understand characters is by what they say. What can you tell about the relationship between Jenna and her dad based on this conversation?

Adam was furious when he was told that he wouldn't be going anywhere after dinner. "I've got places to go and things to do," he protested loudly.

"We know about the things you do," Dad said. Adam glared at Jenna. "She didn't reveal your secret," Dad continued. "The school called. The principal said you're skipping classes. Plus, she said the school has had complaints about you and your new friends being disrespectful to others."

"Someone is complaining about that?" Adam rolled his eyes. "We were just having a little fun."

"You knew what you were doing was wrong," Dad said. "On top of that, you were selfish to ask Jenna to hide your bad behavior."

Adam hung his head. "I never thought about how my actions might affect Jenna."

"I never realized how much power a secret could have," Jenna said. "I never want to keep a secret like this again, agreed?"

"Agreed!" Adam replied.

Academic Vocabulary

Dad said that Jenna did not reveal Adam's secret. How does the context help you understand the meaning of *reveal*?

Unlock the Meaning of the Text

Analyze Characters What clues does the author give you about Jenna, Adam, and Dad? How would you describe each character?

Academic Vocabulary The word *predict* contains the prefix *pre-*, which means "before," and the Latin root *dict*, which means "say." What does this tell you about the meaning of the word *predict*?

How can revealing a secret make it lose its power?
With a partner, discuss how this story helps you understand a secret's power. Then discuss different types of secrets and their effects.

The Benefits of Being Different

Amanda loved learning, especially history and geography. But she wondered if there was any real benefit when it made her different from everyone around her.

Infer Theme

Authors gives clues about the theme, or message, throughout a story. What clues does the author give about the theme of this story in the first two paragraphs?

"You might feel different, but that doesn't mean you shouldn't reveal your intelligence," said Miss Kline, her teacher. "Besides, you wouldn't have qualified for the regional geography competition if you didn't know so much."

"I qualified?" Amanda squealed. "I get to compete against students from all over the region?" Excitement began to mix with concern as she realized she'd be surrounded by other students who loved geography. "Do you think I'll be ready, Miss Kline?" she asked.

"You have time left to prepare, Amanda," Miss Kline replied. "We'll spend the next few weeks reviewing. But you are definitely ready to take part in this competition."

Stepping into the hall, Amanda noticed a noisy group of students moving toward her. At the center of the group was Gary, the school's best soccer player. He was popular in a way she never would be, but he was still nice. He never made fun of her.

"Hey, Amanda," Gary called to her. "What's new?"

"I've qualified for the geography competition," Amanda replied shyly.

"That's great!" Gary responded.

"I don't know why it's such a big deal," a student behind Gary snarled.

Gary spun around and faced the speaker. "Let me illustrate this for you with simple terms. We never beat Central School in anything. If we could beat Central, that would be great. Students from Central will be in this competition. Amanda is smart, and she can beat them."

Amanda blushed, but she knew Gary was right. Her geography knowledge was the best chance Main School had of beating Central at anything.

Gary continued, "I predict that Amanda will bring home the trophy. I don't know about you, but I'll be there cheering for her."

On the day of the competition, Gary was there along with most of the students and teachers from Main School. And Gary's prediction was correct. Amanda did take home the trophy. Being different really paid off.

Academic Vocabulary

One meaning of the word *illustrate* is "to make clear." How does Gary illustrate his point to the other students?

Academic Vocabulary

The prefix *pre-* means "before." What does this tell you about the meaning of the word *predict*?

Unlock the Meaning of the Text

Infer Theme State the story's theme in your own words. List two details that helped you determine the theme.

Academic Vocabulary Synonyms for the word *reveal* include *tell*, *show*, and *expose*. How do these words help you understand the meaning of the word *reveal* in this story?

How can being different be an advantage? Discuss with a partner how the story helped you understand that being different can be an advantage. Then brainstorm ways that your differences help you.

Rewards of a Good Deed

James and Cliff stood in silence at the edge of a yard overgrown with weeds. James held a get-well card that his mother asked him to drop off for their neighbor.

"Mrs. Johnson's yard sure has become a mess since her surgery," said James. He gestured in dismay toward the broken fence. "I guess there's nobody to care for the garden or fix things while she recovers. That's a pity. She's such a kind, generous lady, and her home has always been important to her."

Cliff said, "I wonder if there's some way we could assist her, at least until she's completely healed from her operation. I could repair her fence and pull some weeds."

James replied, "Mrs. Johnson has never had much money. She couldn't pay us for all the work."

"Come on, James," said Cliff. "Haven't you ever heard of charity? Sometimes you just do something because it's the right thing to do. I hope we don't have to be rewarded for doing something good. I like the old, traditional values. You do things just because they're the right thing to do."

The next day, James and Cliff showed up with tools and rakes. As they worked, two more neighbors walked toward the yard. Miss Sanchez held a covered dish. Mr. Robertson carried a toolbox and a ladder.

Academic Vocabulary

What context clues help you understand what Cliff means by *traditional*? What other words might be used to replace *traditional* in this sentence?

James grinned at Cliff. "I worried that people might interpret this as us expecting to be paid. But it looks like other people share your ideas of charity, Cliff."

Miss Sanchez smiled at them. "You have inspired me to cook meals for Mrs. Johnson. I'm going to ask all our neighbors to prepare at least one meal until she has recovered."

Mr. Robertson said, "Thank you for what you are doing here, boys. You've already accomplished so much. I'm going to fix that place on her roof where the shingles have blown off."

"This is exciting," said James. "I predict that more neighbors will catch on to your idea, Cliff. We can do something positive even if there's no reward."

Cliff said, "I wouldn't say there was no reward. Feeling good about your actions is the best reward."

Academic Vocabulary

Interpret means to understand or view something. The word *misinterpret* is made by adding the prefix *mis-*. How does the prefix change the meaning?

Summarize Text

How would you summarize James's feelings? Think about how he felt at the beginning and how he felt at the end.

Unlock the Meaning of the Text

Summarize Text This story takes place over two days. Summarize the events of each day.

Academic Vocabulary Find the word *predict* in the next to last paragraph. The word *predict* means to guess about something that will happen in the future. The suffix *–ion* changes the verb *predict* to the noun *prediction*. Write a sentence using the word *prediction*.

Why should we do good deeds without expecting anything in return? In a small group, discuss how Cliff's comments help you understand how helping others is enough of a reward. Then discuss good deeds you have done and why you did them.

A New Twist to an Old Tale

The other day on the bus, I noticed a woman reading a book of fairy tales. I wanted to grab the book and throw it out the window. Of all the silly things to read, few things are sillier than fairy tales. They all try to teach lessons, but how reliable are they? Take the story of *Cinderella*, for example.

Ever since high school, I've been best friends with Cinderella's older stepsister. Anyone who reads the traditional version of the story thinks Cinderella was lovely and innocent and the stepsisters were horrible. Well, that's one way to interpret what happened. But I was there. The only reason the girls were treated differently is that the stepsisters were nicer. Cinderella was a spoiled brat.

Cinderella says she was mistreated, but that simply isn't true. I don't like to say mean things about anyone, but for her, I'll make an exception. Let's just say Cinderella broke the rules. Her stepsister told me that Cinderella frequently skipped classes and ignored her chores. Instead of cleaning the house, Cinderella lounged around reading fashion magazines. All she talked about was finding and marrying a rich guy. The stepsisters both really disliked Cinderella.

Academic Vocabulary

A *tradition* is a way of doing something year after year. How does this definition help you understand the meaning of the adjective *traditional*?

Infer Theme

The theme of a story is its message about life. How does the narrator's statement "that simply isn't true" help you figure out what the theme of the story will be?

As for not being allowed to go to the prince's ball, that part of the tale is true. But it certainly isn't the whole story. Cinderella had actually been asked to attend. All the girls in the kingdom were invited. Her stepmother had planned to buy Cinderella a beautiful gown. But Cinderella's last report card had been terrible. Naturally her stepmother grounded her. That's the real reason she had to stay home that evening.

But of course she sneaked out of the house and went to the ball anyway. The next thing you knew, Cinderella married the prince and became the queen. She wanted people to write stories about how wonderful she was. She told reporters that her stepsisters and stepmother had treated her badly. It made me crazy to read those stories.

Anyway, you know how fairy tales seem to suggest that good characters get rewarded and bad ones get punished? Clearly, my version of the story reveals that you shouldn't believe everything you read.

Academic Vocabulary

Reveal means "making something known," such as revealing a secret. It also means "open up to view," such as pulling back a curtain. Which meaning is used in the story?

Unlock the Meaning of the Text

Infer Theme What is the story's theme? What details about the characters and plot helped you figure out the theme?

Academic Vocabulary The words *translate*, *clarify*, and *understand* are synonyms for the verb *interpret*. Which synonym helps you understand what it means to *interpret* a version of a story?

How can what we learn from stories guide our actions? In a small group, discuss how this retelling of the Cinderella story can help you decide how to act or what to do.

A Lesson Learned

"You know you're not supposed to take food downstairs," Mom called to Billy. Her trip to his bedroom had revealed several half-eaten meals. She walked into the kitchen carrying the plates with a dried-up sandwich and a half-eaten bags of chips. "When you leave food out, it attracts insects. Insects can carry disease. But even when they don't, no one wants insects in the house. If you're hungry, come upstairs and eat in the kitchen."

"Yes, Mom," Billy said, only half listening. He thought her concerns about insects were silly. The only insects he'd seen in his room were a few harmless little ants. Besides, he didn't mean to leave food out. Sometimes, when he was drawing, he forgot about the food he'd brought downstairs. That made him think, "Maybe I'll illustrate a story about ants and a giant, hairy insect. Then Mom will understand that ants are no big deal."

Billy's mom admired her son's insect illustration, but she did not appreciate his attitude. "I predict that you will discover someday that ants can be a very big deal," Mom said.

Academic Vocabulary

The word *reveal* means "to show or uncover." What did Billy's mom *reveal* in his room?

Academic Vocabulary

Context clues can be found in different sentences. What clues in this paragraph help you understand the word *illustrate*?

Evaluate Details

What details in the first paragraph help you understand why Billy's mom wanted him to keep his room clean?

Billy nodded in agreement, but he really didn't believe what his mom was saying.

A few days later, Billy awoke to a strange, creepy, tickling sensation. He opened his eyes and saw ants crawling over his arm. He jumped out of bed. Ants were scurrying across the floor and in and out of the pretzel bag that was open on his desk. The sandwich he'd left on the table was also covered in ants. Billy ran upstairs, and found his mom.

"Mom!" Billy howled. "There are ants all over my room, even in my bed! There are hundreds of them. I didn't believe what you said. I never imagined this would happen!"

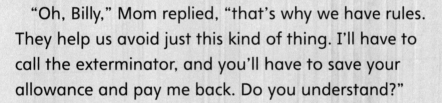

"Oh, Billy," Mom replied, "that's why we have rules. They help us avoid just this kind of thing. I'll have to call the exterminator, and you'll have to save your allowance and pay me back. Do you understand?"

"Yes, Mom. I'm really sorry." Billy had learned his lesson the hard way! The ants had come. And now he would have to use his own money to pay to get the ants removed from his bedroom. Next time, he would listen to his mom.

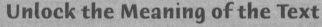

Unlock the Meaning of the Text

Evaluate Details What details in the story helped you understand why Billy should have obeyed the rules?

Academic Vocabulary The Latin root word *dict* means "to say." How does knowing this root word help you understand the meaning of *predict?*

How can being disobedient cause problems? Do you always know the reasons behind rules? In a small group, discuss lessons you have learned about obeying rules. Talk about how the text helps you understand why following the rules is important.

Features

Essential Question

Why is it important to
understand our planet?

PEARSON
realize™
Go ONLINE for
all lessons.

myFocus READER

Read and Interact with Text

Develop comprehension and vocabulary. Make connections.

Finding Earth's Resources

Weekly Question What do we know about Earth's features and processes?

Comprehension Inferences

Academic Vocabulary Context clues

Volcano Lake

Weekly Question In what ways do volcanoes impact Earth?

Comprehension Comprehension

Academic Vocabulary Context clues

How Can We Reduce Pollution?

Weekly Question What daily actions can help reduce pollution?

Comprehension Argument

Academic Vocabulary Root words and affixes

Extreme Locations

Weekly Question What makes an extreme location a place to both protect and explore?

Comprehension Ideas

Academic Vocabulary Shades of meaning

Recycle Island

Weekly Question What happens to what we throw away?

Comprehension Text Evidence

Academic Vocabulary Multiple-meaning words

FINDING EARTH'S
RESOURCES

Academic Vocabulary

How does the rest of the sentence help you to know the meaning of the word *label*?

Pretend you wake up one morning and the year is 2075. Is the world out of resources like gas and clean water? Are people using other kinds of energy like the wind and sun? Does the label on your shirt say *Made from Milk*? If we try to save energy and resources now, the future will be better. Many smart changes are already happening.

Some cities are asking people to get around by bicycle instead of by car. Our air will be cleaner if we drive cars less! Boston has a bikes program. The number of people using bikes in Boston has doubled since it started. Boston added bike paths and parking places for bikes. New York City has plans for a bike-share program. The city has added 250 miles of bike paths. It plans to have places where people can rent bikes. Both programs will make biking easier and safer.

Electric cars can drive longer before they need a charge. A new battery now lets a car go 300 miles on one charge. These cars can help replace gas-powered cars. This will help conserve gas.

Using solar and wind power can save limited resources such as coal and oil. In the past, it took many solar panels to collect the sun's energy. Now we can use flexible solar panels to trap this energy. These panels can be used for roofs and walls. It is easier to collect the sun's energy from large surfaces like these.

We can also make better use of wind power. A new kind of wind machine has been built from fan blades and small engines called generators. These machines change wind into light using clear tubes and LED lights. The light glows through the tubes and lights the ground.

Another hopeful invention is a fabric made from milk! This fabric feels like silk, but it can be washed. And it takes less water to make it than to make cotton. Over 2,500 gallons of water are used to make two pounds of cotton. But amazingly, only a half-gallon of water is needed to make two pounds of fabric. What a difference!

If we save our resources now, we will not face the consequences later. The year 2075 could be a good time to be alive.

Make Inferences

In what ways can using the sun and wind help save our resources? Use details from the text and what you know about resources to help you infer.

Academic Vocabulary

Reactions and *effects* are synonyms for *consequences*. Which synonym fits best in this sentence?

Unlock the Meaning of the Text

Make Inferences Reread the last paragraph. Write inferences telling why 2075 might be a good time. Use details from the text and what you already know.

Academic Vocabulary Read the sixth paragraph with the word *amazingly*. What fact in this paragraph is amazing? How does this help you understand the word *amazingly*?

What do we know about Earth's features and resources? Talk with a partner about how the text helped you learn more about Earth's features and resources. Then talk about ways you can save resources everyday.

Volcano Lake

What pictures come to mind when you think of a volcano? Maybe you think of melted lava gushing. Maybe you see smoke rising in the sky and ash on the ground. You probably don't think of a beautiful lake with clear, blue water, though, do you?

Thousands of years ago, a volcano named Mount Mazama erupted, or blew up. The top of the volcano fell in and formed a bowl-shaped pit called a crater. Lava sealed the bottom. Over time, snow melted and rain fell. As a consequence, the crater filled up with water. It is now called Crater Lake.

Crater Lake is one of the deepest lakes in the world, but it is not easy to find. If you went hiking in the Cascade mountains of Oregon, you could look for this hidden treasure. It is hidden by the walls of the old volcano. The walls tower above the lake, from 500 to 2,000 feet. At its widest spot, Crater Lake is about six miles across.

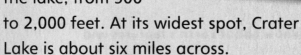

Academic Vocabulary

The word *consequence* can mean "a punishment, or a bad result from an action." It can also mean "something that logically flows from an action or condition." Which fits best in this sentence?

Monitor Comprehension

As you read, ask yourself why the lake is hard to find. What details help you know the reason it is a hidden lake?

Crater Lake is known for its bright blue color. The water color is intense because the lake is very deep. In fact, this lake was once called Deep Blue Lake. No rivers or streams flow into the lake so the water stays clean and pure.

If you visit Crater Lake, you will notice two islands: Wizard Island and Phantom Ship. You may also see a thirty-foot tall log floating upright in the lake. What's so special about this log? It's been named the "Old Man" of Crater Lake! This log has been floating around the lake for over one hundred years!

Today, the area where Crater Lake sits is called Crater Lake National Park. The lake and the bordering land have been protected and preserved since 1902. Tourists can enjoy camping, fishing, and hiking during the warm months. From October to June, the park is often buried under snow. No matter the season, Crater Lake is always a place of great beauty.

Academic Vocabulary

If you remove the *-ing* ending, you see the root word, *border*. How does this help you understand the word *bordering*?

Unlock the Meaning of the Text

Monitor Comprehension Nonfiction texts have a lot of details. Make a list of all of the details about Crater Lake and use them to draw a picture of the area.

Academic Vocabulary What does the word *preserved* mean in the last paragraph? What other word in that sentence helped you know the meaning?

In what ways do volcanoes impact Earth? Discuss with a partner how this text helps you understand how volcanoes can affect Earth. What have you learned about other ways volcanoes can impact Earth?

How Can We Reduce Pollution?

When people talk about pollution, they are talking about things that make land, water, or air dirty and less safe. Pollution is bad for our Earth.

Reports about pollution might show pictures of smoke coming from factories. They might also show pipes pouring wastewater into a lake. However, one of the most common forms of pollution is litter. People are amazed to learn how much litter can hurt our world.

Litter is the trash people toss on the ground or leave behind. It can be plastic bottles, paper bags, gum wrappers, or empty cups. It may not seem like much to the person tossing it, but the trash adds up.

The consequences of littering include making things look dirty and messy. However, there are many other bad effects. Litter pollution can make places less safe for plants, animals, and people.

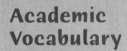

Academic Vocabulary

Synonyms for *amazed* include *surprised* and *shocked*. How does this help you understand the word? What are people amazed by in this paragraph?

Academic Vocabulary

The Latin word *sequi* means "to follow." This Latin root can help you find the meaning of *consequences*: the results that follow from an action. What are consequences of littering?

Litter can hurt birds and animals. They choke on old chewing gum or get trapped in plastic bags. They get caught in the plastic holders from packs of soda cans. Plants get covered up by litter and don't get the sun they need to grow.

Litter can clog drains and sewers, and they stop working. It can make parks and beaches unsafe for children and families. Sometimes, people help pick up litter for free. But it costs money to clean up drains and sewers. And then more money is needed to rescue the animals hurt by litter.

This is sad because litter is a type of pollution that is easy to stop. Don't throw your food wrappers, lunch bags, or plastic bottles on the ground. If you have a picnic, clean everything up to preserve Earth.

Research has shown that the problem of litter pollution can be solved only by individuals. Each person must be responsible for his or her actions. This can mean cleaning up our neighborhoods. But it also means never littering. Tell your friends. And decide for yourself that you will never again throw litter on the ground. This could put an end to litter pollution for good.

Analyze Argument

What details does the writer include to convince the reader that small, everyday actions can make a big difference?

Unlock the Meaning of the Text

Analyze Argument The author talks about the effects of litter on Earth. Make a list of three details that support the author's argument.

Academic Vocabulary The Latin *servare* means "keep or guard." We see this Latin root in the word *preserve*, which means "to keep safe." Look up the word *conserve* in a dictionary to see how these words are related.

What daily actions can help reduce pollution? In a small group, discuss how reading the text helped you understand how to prevent pollution. Then discuss ways in which you can reduce litter pollution where you live.

EXTREME LOCATIONS

People love places that are extreme: tallest mountains, deepest parts of the ocean, highest waterfalls. Earth has many extreme places. There are places that have the hottest weather, or the coldest. Other places are the wettest, driest, or windiest. People like to learn about these places.

Africa, Asia, and Australia are all home to very hot locations. However, the United States is the location of the place that holds the record for highest temperature. That place is Death Valley. Death Valley is on the border between two states. They are California and Nevada. The highest temperature ever recorded there was 134 degrees. I bet it isn't a surprise that Death Valley is a desert!

You might think that no one would visit such a hot place. However, Death Valley is a popular place to visit. Unusual plants and animals, as well as rocks in pretty formations, make it a great place to explore. It is a national park, so there are park rangers who can tell visitors about Death Valley. Park rangers also make sure people stay safe in the heat. Death Valley can be both dangerous and beautiful.

Another extreme place is Antarctica. This place holds the record for the coldest temperature ever recorded. That record was 136 degrees below zero. It never gets warm enough to go outside without a coat in Antarctica. But Antarctica has something in common with Death Valley. Both are deserts! That is because it is too cold to rain in Antarctica.

Scientists who study these places are amazed by what they have found. In Death Valley, seeds can wait for years for rain. When the rains do come, plants begin to sprout, and soon the desert floor is covered with bright flowers. Death Valley is the hottest place on Earth, but it still can freeze in the winter. In Antarctica, penguins raise their young on fields of ice. Fossils of trees and leaves have been discovered under the ice. Scientists can only wonder what other surprises they will uncover.

People saw long ago that it was important to preserve these extreme places. There are places all around the world that are being preserved. This makes sure that these places will be here for the people of the future to study and explore.

Academic Vocabulary

The verb *preserve* means "to protect or keep safe." The noun *preserve* means "a place set aside to protect natural resources." How are these meanings related?

Unlock the Meaning of the Text

Explain Ideas What does the text tell you about extreme places on Earth? What makes these places extreme? Find details in the text to help you explain the idea.

Academic Vocabulary The word *amazed* means "to be surprised," or "to be filled with wonder." What details can you list about these extreme places that have scientists *amazed*?

What makes an extreme location a place both to protect and to explore? With a partner, discuss how the text supports the idea that people should protect extreme places. Then talk about whether you would explore Death Valley or Antarctica and why.

Recycled Island

Academic Vocabulary

A *label* describes or gives a name to something. The word can be a verb or a noun. How can you tell that it is a noun here?

Recycling isn't a new idea. It is just a new label for an old idea. People have always found ways to make something new from something old.

In today's world, we hear a lot about recycling. People recycle cans, paper, and plastic bottles to reduce the amount of trash that we have to bury. Many people are trying to do more recycling. They want to make sure the planet is still a nice place to live in the future. But some people recycle more than others.

Would you believe that someone could create an entire island as a way of recycling products? It's true. Richart Sowa is an artist from England. In 1998, he began building an island near the coast of Mexico. He called it Spiral Island. The island floated on top of about 250,000 empty plastic bottles. Unfortunately, a hurricane destroyed Spiral Island in 2005. Most of the island washed up on the nearby beach.

Use Text Evidence to Explain Events

Find the details in the text that explain why mangroves were planted on the island.

However, this did not end Sowa's dream. He began building a new island in 2007. He again gathered thousands of plastic bottles to keep the island afloat. As he did with the first island, Sowa planted a garden, bushes, and trees. Some of the trees are fruit trees, but many are mangroves. Mangroves have underwater root systems. Sowa knew that the roots would weave together and provide a strong base for his island. Since mangroves hold sand in place, they helped the island grow. It is now more than sixty feet across.

Three beaches now make up part of the island's border.

Sowa continues to improve his floating home. He used bamboo and plywood from trash piles to construct a two-story house. He also created a solar-powered waterfall and a wave-powered washing machine. Mirrors inside a clear barrel use the sun's rays to heat water. Sowa has a boat made from plastic bottles, so he can go to shore. He also welcomes tourists who are interested in the island.

Some call the island the perfect design for the future. Others wonder how long it will last. One of the consequences of living in a place with hurricanes is that the island could be in danger. What if a storm destroyed this island again? Could plastic bottles litter nearby beaches? Sowa came up with a clever way of recycling trash. Maybe, in the future, he will also find a way to protect his island from hurricanes.

Academic Vocabulary

A *consequence* is "an effect or result that naturally follows an action." What words in the definition help you understand the word *consequences*?

Unlock the Meaning of the Text

Use Text Evidence to Explain Events What reasons are given to explain why Sowa built the island? Make a list of the details you find in the text.

Academic Vocabulary The word *border* can mean "an outer edge of something." It can also mean "a decorative edge on paper." Which definition applies here?

What happens to what we throw away? In a small group, discuss how reading the text helped you think about where things go when they are thrown away. Then talk about things that you can recycle.

Acknowledgments

Photographs

Photo locators denoted as follows Top (T), Center (C), Bottom (B), Left (L), Right (R), Background (Bkgd)

4 Grigorii Pisotsckii/Shutterstock, **6** (Bkgrd) Leigh Prather/Fotolia, (TR) Library of Congress Prints and Photographs Division Washington, D.C. 20540, Reproduction Number: LC-DIG-ggbain-24288, **7** PA Images/Alamy Stock Photo, **8** (Bkgrd) Jeremyreds/Fotolia, (BR) Paolo Gallo/Fotolia, **9** Tesgro Tessieri/Fotolia, **10** (Bkgrd) Chris Amaral/Thinkstock/Fotolia, (BR) David Lyons/Alamy Stock Photo, **12** (Bkgrd) GeorgeManga/Getty Images, (BL) Daniel Loncarevic/Fotolia, **13** (CR) Jupiterimages/Thinkstock/Getty Images, (TR) dell/Fotolia, **14** (Bkgrd) Iakov Kalinin/Fotolia, (CL) John D. Simmons/KRT/Newscom, (TCL) Neo Edmund/ Fotolia, (TR) Denys Prykhodov/Fotolia, **15** (BL) Lee Snider/Alamy Stock Photo, (TR) Fotolia, **16** Puhhha/Shutterstock, **18** John P. Kelly/Getty Images, (TR) Dneprstock/Shutterstock; **20** (Bkgrd) Nasi_lemak/Shutterstock, (T) Thinkstock/Getty Images, **21** (BR) Incredible Arctic/ Fotolia, (CR) Incredible Arctic/Fotolia, (TR) Uryadnikov Sergey/Fotolia, **22** (Bkgrd) M'Rio/ Shutterstock, (BR) Scott Harms/Fotolia, (CR) Rusty Dodson/Fotolia, (TR) Arman/Fotolia, **23** (BR) JLindsay/Fotolia, (TCR) Okea/Fotolia, (TR) Steve Byland/Fotolia, **24** (Bkgrd) cynoclub/ Fotolia, (BL) JLindsay/Fotolia, (TR) cynoclub/Fotolia, **25** Lars Christensen/Shutterstock, (CR) Lorenzo Buttitta/Fotolia, **26** (Bkgrd) Kanunnikov Pavel/Shutterstock, (BL) dlugoska/Fotolia, (BR) wernerrieger/Fotolia, (CL) Cathy Keifer/Fotolia, (TR) John Foxx/Thinkstock/Getty Images, **27** (BR) Fotolia/Fotolia, (CR) Danny Wolin/Fotolia, (TR) fivespots/Fotolia, **28** Jim West/ Alamy Stock Photo, **30** (Bkgrd) Galyna Andrushko/Fotolia, (B) Douglas Graham/Roll Call/ Newscom, (TR) National Archives, **32** (B) lunamarina/Fotolia, (BL) Ariel Skelley/Getty Images, **33** (CR) Saskia Massink/Fotolia, (TR) cphoto/Fotolia, **34** (Bkgrd) Jupiterimages/Thinkstock/ Getty Images, (B) Studio Gi/Fotolia, (CR) Library of Congress Prints and Photographs Division Washington, D.C. 20540, Reproduction Number: LC-DIG-ppmsca-09571, 034 TR Library of Congress Prints and Photographs Division Washington, D.C. 20540, Reproduction Number: LC-USZ62-54231, **35** ® Jupiterimages/Thinkstock/Getty Images, (TR) Odile Noel/Lebrecht Music and Arts Photo Library/Alamy Stock Photo, **36** (Bkgrd) kenzo/Fotolia, (BL) rgbspace/Fotolia, **37** (BR) dzain/Fotolia, (TR) Fotolia/Fotolia, **38** (Bkgrd) Ferenc Szelepcsenyi/Fotolia, (BR) tiero/ Fotolia, **40** Elgreko/Shutterstock, **42** (B) Tomas Rodriguez/Getty Images, **44** Stockbroker/MBI/ Alamy Stock Photo, **45** Jamesteohart/Shutterstock, **46** Inti St Clair/Getty Images, **48** (Bkgrd) red2000/Fotolia, (BC) Volha Drabovich/Fotolia, (BL) Travis Manley/Fotolia, (TR) ksena32/ Fotolia, **49** (B) Loraliu/Fotolia, (TL) Kirill Bodrov/Fotolia, **50** (Bkgrd) donatas1205/Fotolia, (B) Tupungato/Fotolia, (BR) Jim Barber/Fotolia, (CL) Judex/Fotolia, (L) Hemera Technologies/ Thinkstock/Getty Images, **51** Brad Pict/Fotolia, **52** Romolo Tavani/Shutterstock, **54** (Bkgrd) LeonART l/Shutterstock, (BL) lassedesignen/Fotolia, (TR) VitalyTitov/Fotolia, **55** Stratenschulte Julian/DPA/ABACA/Newscom, **56** (Bkgrd) PhotographyByMK/Fotolia, (BCR) GVictoria/Fotolia, (C) scol22/Fotolia, (CR) DOC RABE Media/Fotolia, **57** (B) Nataliya Peregudova/Fotolia, (TR) dendron/Fotolia, **58** Chris Howes/Wild Places Photography/Alamy Stock Photo, **59** (Bkgrd) Paladin12/Shutterstock, (CR) Alfa Photostudio/Shutterstock, **60** Dan Suzio/Science Source, **61** Rebecca Yale/Getty Images, **62** (Bkgrd) Aggie 11/Shutterstock, (BR) Roger Cracknell 01/ classic/Alamy Stock Photo, **63** Evan Lorne/Shutterstock.